Decorative Ironwork

Decorative Ironwork

Umberto Zimelli and Giovanni Vergerio

Paul Hamlyn

LONDON · NEW YORK · SYDNEY · TORONTO

Translated by Anthony Sutton from the Italian original

Il ferro battuto

© 1966 Fratelli Fabbri Editori, Milan

This edition © copyright 1969
THE HAMLYN PUBLISHING GROUP LIMITED
LONDON · NEW YORK · SYDNEY · TORONTO
Hamlyn House, Feltham, Middlesex, England

S.B.N. 60001228x

Text filmset in Great Britain by
Keyspools Ltd, Golborne

Printed in Italy by
Fratelli Fabbri Editori, Milan

Contents

IRON IN ANTIQUITY

Iron was extremely rare in the ancient civilisations of the Eastern Mediterranean. The Egyptians, the Phoenicians, the Jews and the peoples of the Aegean used successively weapons or tools of stone, bone, copper and bronze (which had probably been discovered by pure chance). The rarity of iron explains its use in ornaments, along with gold, silver, precious stones and enamels. Therefore we cannot properly speak of the working of iron in the sense of the term employed today. It was more a matter of utilising a very rare metal to make various small implements—scalpels, graving tools, chisels—which are indispensable in the working of stone, marble, alabaster, wood and precious metals; iron tools could be used with far greater precision than tools of stone, copper or bronze.

Flinders Petrie, O. Montelius and other distinguished archaeologists agree that the Egyptians knew about iron more than three millennia before Christ; this was first demonstrated in 1881, by Maspero's discovery of six iron scalpels used as early as 3500 BC inside a room of the pyramid of Unas, near Saqqara. But the same archaeologists declare that it was a long time before the metal was used extensively. This seems to have occurred under Rameses II (19th dynasty), in whose tomb were found axes, daggers and other weapons of iron.

It thus seems reasonably well established that the Iron Age in Egypt began in about 1200 BC. The mineral probably came from Syria, which supplied all the other civilisations of the Near East. Assyria may have been the first country to discover how to produce iron, but if so it was nonetheless unable to use it continuously or in quantity before the 12th century BC. For centuries, incorruptible bronze was more important than iron, which was an easy prey to rust, difficult to produce, and therefore costly. In their poems, Homer and Hesiod speak of it as relatively rare; and later, in the Imperial Roman period,

Pliny the Elder relates that in his day iron was dearer than silver.

All the same, the slow but continuous progress of metallurgy, which was favoured by more efficient use of charcoal at a high temperature, enabled men to produce ever greater quantities of iron. The metal now became indispensable in the creation and development of a civilisation. The Etruscans at Populonia worked copper and bronze with incomparable skill. They also extracted a large quantity of iron from the island of Elba and mines on the mainland, and worked and smelted it for many centuries; a visible testimony to this are the colossal mounds of slag and refuse from the Etruscan furnaces which are deposited on the coast at Porto Baratti. All over the world, iron was gradually being extracted, smelted and hammered. All the great civilisations of later Antiquity—Greece, Etruria, Rome—benefited from using this strong and ductile metal, and it gradually replaced copper and bronze as the material from which objects for practical use were made, supplying tools for the arts, the crafts and farm work, and weapons for attack and defence. The craft of the blacksmith became a 'mystery', with its own trade secrets and traditions; and the prominence of black-smiths in myth and legend is an indication of the awe with which men regarded the worker in metal. Both northern and Mediterranean Europe possessed blacksmith gods: the Scandinavians worshipped Thor of the great hammer and iron gloves, the Greeks and Romans Hephaestus-Vulcan, who forged the armour of Achilles and built the palaces of Olympus.

But these peoples, who worked every other more or less precious metal in such a masterly way, did not use iron to create works of art. Many centuries passed from the beginning of the Iron Age—centuries which saw the birth, efflorescence and decay of kingdoms and empires: Egypt, Assyria, Greece, Etruria. Thousands of magnificent objects made in antiquity have been found and preserved in galleries and museums in every part of the world, and every day they are still being discovered: objects of copper, bronze, clay, ivory, gold, silver, wood and even cloth. But almost nothing of iron, let alone of artistic work in iron: only formless splinters and pinches of reddish powder.

1. Window. 11th century. Monastery of Sta Maria del Solario, Brescia.

1.   Window. 11th century. Monastery of Sta Maria del Solario, Brescia. An example of a primitive grille made of vertical and horizontal bars held together by rings.

2.   Portal of St Anne. 13th century. Notre-Dame, Paris. A wonderful example of ironwork superimposed on a wooden portal. The old crude iron strap which reinforces the wooden structure has been refined so that it appears purely decorative. The ironwork has been embossed and engraved, and the large decorated scrolls interweave with other spiral decorations in the shape of volutes, leaves and rosettes.

3.   Grille from the Abbey of Ourscamp. 13th century. Musée Le Secq des Tournelles, Rouen. This grille, one of the master-pieces of Gothic ironwork, surpasses even the doors of Notre-Dame; it was technically a far more difficult piece of work to execute.

4.   Door with ironwork. 13th century. St Paul's Cathedral, Liège. The ironwork provides the decoration on this door. The scroll motifs are ultimately derived from the decoration on illuminated manuscripts.

2.   Portal of St Anne. 13th century. Notre-Dame, Paris.

3. Grille from the Abbey of Ourscamp. 13th
century. Musée Le Secq des Tournelles, Rouen.

4.   Door with ironwork. 13th century. St Paul's Cathedral,
Liège.

The reason for this strange lacuna has been a subject of debate. Some have argued that the rapidity with which iron becomes oxidised accounts for the disappearance of antique objects; others point out that no mineral leaves such lasting traces as iron. The most likely explanation is that it was extraordinarily difficult to obtain iron that could be worked by the hammer; and that the few fragments used as ornaments came from tiny quantities that cropped up on the surface of the earth.

Human experience in the complex task of working iron continued to accumulate despite the rise and fall of empires. Certainly there were periods of greater or lesser activity in consequence of political upheavals; but ironworking steadily created a new civilisation and new necessities. The skill of the smith furnished handicraft and agriculture with many useful objects, and also began to be applied to building. Supporting metal straps to locks, hinges, fastenings, handles, door-knockers, grilles, etc. mark the modest beginnings of artistic wrought-iron work.

For the purposes of the present study, the collapse of the Roman Empire and the Barbarian migrations must be passed over. The history of wrought-iron recommences with the return to order (albeit precarious) that gave birth to a new civilisation. From the beginning of the 11th to the beginning of the 13th century, art is usually referred to as 'Romanesque'. The term is inaccurate, for the substratum of Roman culture, though intensely admired, was adapted and transformed by the peoples of Europe.

THE ROMANESQUE AGE

Roman styles had influenced the peoples of Europe in a number of ways; but until the emergence of the Romanesque, Roman, Christian and Barbarian elements had never been synthesised into a single unique style.

The advent of Christianity during the 1st century had brought people of different races into a common brotherhood. It had offered them new figurative elements, new symbols and a very suggestive iconography with which to replace a flagging pagan tradition. But religious unification had not brought

5. Firescreen. 13th century. Musée Le Secq des Tournelles, Rouen.

6. Tomb of Cansignorio della Scala. Detail of the screen.
14th century. Verona.

5.   Firescreen. 13th century. Musée Le Secq des Tournelles, Rouen. A piece of beautiful and harmonious composition. The scrolls spring from bundles of thick bars like tree-trunks, and interweave and dissolve with wonderful fluency.

6.   Tomb of Cansignorio della Scala. Detail of the screen. 14th century. Verona. Each tomb of the monumental sepulchral complex of the Scaligeri is enclosed by a screen whose pre-dominating motif is formed by a quatrefoil with the heraldic 'ladder' of the family in the centre. The tomb shown here is dated 1380.

7.   Tomb of Cansignorio della Scala. Full view. 14th century. Verona. This group of the Scaligeran tombs is surrounded by a wrought-iron screen whose ornamental motif is constantly repeated. These screens are perhaps the best-known wrought-iron works in the world.

7. Tomb of Cansignorio della Scala. Full view. 14th
century. Verona.

about a unified artistic idiom, and the peoples of Europe were therefore able to interpret the great themes of Christianity in their own manner.

The development of 11th-century art is closely connected with the increasing influence and power of the Church. The minor arts in particular flourished as a result of clerical patronage, and the period witnessed the birth of many technical advances. Marvellous effects were obtained from different materials, and religious art of unsurpassed beauty was produced by goldsmiths, by founders and craftsmen who worked copper and bronze, and (not least) by black-smiths.

The principal seats of ecclesiastical life were the monasteries, and in particular those where bishops resided, and it was there that schools and workshops developed and the best craftsmen from all over Europe came to learn their trade. Ecclesiastics themselves sometimes helped to execute works they had commissioned.

In the course of time, the prosperity and consequent growth of towns gave lay craftsmen an opportunity to develop their skill, and they began to introduce elements taken from popular art, which had retained its vitality. The gradual laicising of art brought about many changes in style and technique; and the workshops of the monasteries slowly declined.

In the Romanesque period, the most notable product of the blacksmith's art was the ironwork made for doors, which reached the highest standards of technical skill. The spaces between bars were often filled with open-work: crosses, rosettes, rings, interlacing designs and heraldic animals. There is a fine example of tendrils on the 13th-century door of the Cathedral of St Paul at Liège (plate 4) on which there is a spiral motif similar to that on the lateral doors of Notre-Dame in Paris (plate 2).

Germany. The 12th-century screen in the crypt of Hildesheim Cathedral is given remarkable grace by its multiform motifs and the delightful symmetry of its composition. The C-shaped scrolls have been elongated and juxtaposed; they are placed between the vertical bars, to which they are bound and welded. Inside the scrolls are a variety of motifs: palmettes, pierced rosettes, quatrefoils, fleurs-de-lis and even little birds. The whole is enclosed by a frame culminating in an arch at the top. The gate at Lüneburg is similar, but the motifs within the C are less varied.

The door of the Cathedral at Erfurt is of a different type. The iron decoration is created by flat bands, with sparse reliefs in the rosettes but with a great display of bosses all along the shafts; the ramifications are in decorated scrolls and rosettes. This has been done in such a way that the ironwork is given great vigour. The door is also singular in that it has a different design on each leaf: floral on one, almost geometrical on the other. The effect is very fine.

England. The strapwork on the door of Ely Cathedral bears a resemblance to the ironwork of French and German doors in certain decorative details, and in its construction and technique. But it is quite different in the simplicity of its design and its ornamentation, in the form of large scrolls and whorls terminating in rosettes and palmettes.

France. The wooden portal with ironwork at St Trophime in Arles has more elaborately worked

8. Screen of the Rinuccini Chapel. 14th century. Basilica of S. Croce, Florence.

8.   Screen of the Rinuccini Chapel. 14th century. Basilica
of S. Croce, Florence. A classic example of a Gothic screen
(1371) by Sienese master smiths. The semicircular arch, into
which very elegant mullioned windows are inserted, constitutes
the dynamic element.

9.   Detail of the screen in the Rinuccini Chapel. 14th century.
Basilica of S. Croce, Florence. This detail shows the original
decorative solution arrived at by the makers; it is mainly done
by employing Gothic architectural elements. Notice the re-
finement and elegance of the columns.

10.   Screen. 15th century. Palazzo Pubblico, Siena. This
large screen (of Sienese craftsmanship) is an example of the
harmonious use of the quatrefoil motif. The frieze in pierced
and embossed sheet-metal enriches the upper section.

11.   Detail of the screen in plate 10. 15th century. Palazzo
Pubblico, Siena. The decorative motif of the lower part
witnesses the triumph of the emblem motif of 'Flamboyant'
Gothic. The cresting has been fashioned with flowers and
halberd-heads.

9. Detail of the screen in the Rinuccini Chapel. 14th century. Basilica of S. Croce, Florence.

10. Screen. 15th century. Palazzo Pubblico, Siena.

11. Detail of screen. 15th century. Palazzo Pubblico,
Siena.

decoration but does not compare with the doors of Notre-Dame in Paris. Each of the two leaves has three horizontal bolts springing from the hinges and flowering into volutes and palmettes terminating in a point shaped like a fleur-de-lis.

Spain. In the Middle Ages, Spain was a region of considerable artistic importance. The southern part of the peninsula was ruled by the Moors and produced art in Eastern styles. French influence was strong in the north, and important works in the Romanesque style were produced during the 11th and 12th centuries. The 12th-century portal of the Abbey of Marcevols in Northern Spain demonstrates how wooden doors were reinforced and at the same time decorated by ironwork appliances, hinges and bolts. The 'door' of the Cathedral at Palencia is really a grille enclosed in a wooden frame, and it is possible to see through the close-knit web of delicate scrolls fastened by collars and vertical bars.

Between about 1150 and 1225, when the power and the authority of the Holy Roman Empire was declining, an important political change took place in Europe which directly influenced the development of the arts. France became the greatest of the powers, thanks to the shrewd policy of her monarchy. One result was that the French style of the mid-12th century had been universally diffused and adopted within a few years: the Gothic style.

THE GOTHIC STYLE

The term '12th-century Renaissance' is often used to describe the awakening of Europe at the beginning of the High Middle Ages. A new freedom of conception and expression appeared in literature and thought (in, for example, the works of Chrétien de Troyes and Peter Abelard), and found its visual equivalent in the Gothic style. Romanesque architecture, with its emphasis on mass, was replaced by a dynamic linear style which soon manifested itself in the other visual arts.

This was a great period for the art of wrought-ironwork. At first it was applied to strapwork, locks and grilles. The straps terminating in a leaf-shape were enlivened with open-work, and later with reliefs. The locks of the fastenings used in Germany terminated mostly in axe-heads; the door-knockers and handles were lightly decorated in open-work.

Iron grilles in Spain and Western Germany were mainly constructed of vertical bars, sometimes with a few transverse links twisted around them; whereas in Eastern Germany grilles made by bars crossing each other were preferred.

A different technique from the work fashioned on flat bands was preferred in France; a technique which entailed the forging of cusps, little temples, baldachins and even little figures of saints in high relief. In the 13th century, the art of French smiths thus reached a standard appropriate to the splendour of French Gothic cathedrals, the portals and fastenings of which were adorned with works of rare beauty and craftsmanship.

Examples of these incomparable works of art are the magnificent portal of Notre-Dame in Paris and the masterpiece from the Abbey of Ourscamp (plate 3). The latter is of greater technical importance, for it is not ironwork applied to a wooden door (as at Notre-Dame) but an independent iron gate with two leaves.

12. Plate for a door-handle. 15th century. Germanisches
Nationalmuseum, Nuremberg.

13. Lock. 15th or 16th century. Victoria and Albert Museum, London.

14. Tabernacle grille. 15th century. Spitalkirche, Krems.

12. Plate for a door-handle. 15th century. Germanisches Nationalmuseum, Nuremberg. This is in pierced and engraved iron; it comes from the church at Blutemburg. Decorations of this type are numerous, especially in Austria and Germany, and are applied to locks, door-knockers, door-handles and hinges.

13. Lock. 15th or 16th century. Victoria and Albert Museum, London. An example of French Gothic, one of the great periods of wrought-ironwork: it was applied to strapwork, locks, hinges and window grilles. A striking effect was often obtained by adding a few motifs in high relief.

14. Tabernacle grille. 15th century. Spitalkirche, Krems. Pierced, embossed and chased wrought-iron. The massive panel has been cleverly lightened by the open-work of thirty-five of the panels. Hunting scenes alternate with Christian monograms, variously rendered, and scenes from the Passion.

15. Screen. 16th century. Royal Chapel, Granada Cathedral. (Ediciones Agata) A monumental work of classical design, the masterpiece of the Spanish ironsmiths. It is divided into three orders and supported by columns and thick vertical twisted bars. The cresting is composed of decorated scrolls, berries and acanthus leaves.

15. Screen. 16th century. Royal Chapel, Granada Cathedral.

Also worth seeing is the splendid firescreen in the Musée Le Secq des Tournelles at Rouen (plate 5). If the attribution to the 13th century is accepted, it may be regarded as a development of the aesthetic taste displayed in the iron grille at the Musée de Cluny; and in another 13th-century grille, in the Cathedral of Le Puy, which is constructed of bars in square sections with sharp angles, partly pierced.

The portal of the Cathedral of St Gilles is in the same style as that of Notre-Dame but much simpler in design, with a decoration of leaves and convolvuli. The ironwork on the portal of St Paul's at Liège is in higher relief and the iron has been treated with greater harshness.

The decorative inspiration of all these works is clearly derived from the illuminated manuscripts of the period.

Germany. The door in the Germanisches National-museum at Nuremberg is divided into three sections, two reserved for the supporting strapwork of the hinges, and the third, central section that is purely decorative. The bands are now actually worked in a filigree pattern with tiny whorls carrying still smaller palmettes and microscopic tendrils. The central panel is divided into lozenge shapes, and is also very finely engraved. Every space contains heraldic figures: dragons, rampant lions, eagles and so on. The work is like some masterpiece of the jeweller's art, made in iron by masters of extraordinary skill. The effect is somewhat artificial, perhaps because the forge, the anvil, the hammer and the ardour of the smith are felt to be missing.

Among the more beautiful works in the late Gothic style is the trellis work above the baptismal font at Antwerp with its wonderful naturalistic branches and foliage; and the iron pulpit at Feldkirch (Vorarlberg), which was at first intended for another purpose. It is a complicated structure enlivened by figures in painted wood which represent the Jews collecting manna in the desert. The upper part, which resembles a tower, appears to have affinities with the tabernacle of the Blessed Sacrament in the Church of St Lawrence at Nuremberg.

Lamp-holders are transformed in various ways by Gothic artists. The one in the cathedral at Magdeburg has a turret motif; others have a figure, a shrine or a tower in the centre, from which several bracket-arms spring out in daring and elegant curves. A beautiful example of this type is the lamp-holder in the eastern choir of Augsburg Cathedral, dating from the beginning of the 14th century.

ITALY IN THE MIDDLE AGES

Medieval Italian art developed in conditions quite different from those prevailing in the countries beyond the Alps, partly because the influence of the ancient world remained so strong and partly because vigorous and independent urban communities developed so early. There are references to corporations and guilds as properly constituted, active organisations before the 11th century. The Guild of the Marzeri, for example, had been active in the Venetian Republic since 942, and was composed of eight trades, including 'the tinsmiths, the scale-makers, the iron workers and the lead workers'. And it is recorded that in 1030 a blacksmith, Giovanni Sagornino of Venice, complained to Doge Pietro Barbolano about the steward of the Guild of Smiths.

16. Spanish screen. 16th century. Musée du Louvre, Paris.

16.   Spanish screen. 16th century. Musée du Louvre, Paris. The uprights are of solid iron; the rest of the grille is in open-work on embossed sheet-iron. These works in the 'Flamboyant' Gothic style are constructed with motifs taken from architecture.

17.   Spanish coffer. 16th century. Museo Arqueológico Nacional, Madrid. Notice the extremely complicated lock, the work of an experienced, highly skilled craftsman with superb decorative taste.

18.   Choir gate. 16th century. Augsburg Cathedral. The decorative motif of the C-scroll covering the framework indicates the influence of the Italian Renaissance, but the cresting reveals the German Gothic origin of the work.

19.   Detail of the balustrade at the sides of the gate. 16th century. Augsburg Cathedral. German Gothic ironcraft is even more evident in these panels. The rods pass through metal eyelets at the intersections, and the palmettes and buds are in Gothic style.

17. Spanish coffer. 16th century. Museo Arqueológico Nacional, Madrid.

18. Choir gate. 16th century. Augsburg Cathedral.

19. Detail of the balustrade at the sides of the gate. 16th
century. Augsburg Cathedral.

Arrow-makers, armourers, weapon-makers, swordsmiths, spurriers and farriers have given their names to streets, squares and districts in every town of Italy. But blacksmiths were more than weapon-makers. They were called *magistri clavari* ('master locksmiths') because they were skilled in constructing keys and locks; and they also made coffers, door-hinges, strapwork to reinforce and decorate doors, door-plates, richly worked door-knockers, etc.

The rings (*campanelle*) to which waiting horses were tied were useful little objects of iron. The story of the 'Column of Hospitality' (which still stands in the centre of the Castle of Bertinoro) is an interesting illustration of medieval courtesy. It is related that on this column were fixed as many halter rings as there were noble families residing in the district. A traveller passing the castle could tie his horse to any one of the halter rings 'and according to the decree of Fate, he was led to the house of the noble gentleman to whom this ring belonged, and honoured as befitted his rank.'

By the beginning of the 13th century, wrought-iron work was starting to flourish throughout Italy;

and artistic intentions were gradually formed—a desire to beautify even the most humble object. It was in the workshops of medieval craftsmen that the Renaissance was born, and it was through the direct experience gained in the crafts that artists acquired a plastic language capable of being used to create masterpieces of architecture, painting and sculpture. While the guild system flourished, no artist was able to make a living outside the workshops: all had to work their way from apprentice to master. The workshops were the schools of art.

Siena was one of the first Italian towns to produce works of art in wrought iron, and from her workshops came the first objects that retained in the forging of the iron the natural characteristics of this strong and raw material. Humble and useful objects were conceived with an ingenuous imaginativeness and executed with genuine spontaneity. A lamp made at the beginning of the 13th century was not forged from blocks of iron (as was to be the case during the Renaissance); it was made by bending bars and small plates, and riveting them together in a rather primitive fashion. It is astonishing that

Italian feeling for proportion could triumph in spite of the patchwork method that might so easily have made the final product look a jumble.

One of the most appreciated qualities in the art of ironworking is skill in drawing forth as much work as possible from a single block of iron. This seems an opportune moment to quote a theorist of the last century, Gottfried Sempers: 'Form should result from the material, from the technique and from the final purpose'—a dictum which is valid for all human work.

The Sienese workshops produced works that were unpretentious but beautiful and useful: hooks and spikes, rings—often decorated—for tethering horses, lamps, supporting brackets, fire-dogs, lanterns, hand-hammers and thousands of other objects in common use.

Soon, however, Sienese smiths had an opportunity to apply their technical mastery to more important works. One example is the monumental screen in the collegiate church at Bobbio. The dominating motif is similar to that of the door of the cathedral at Palencia, which has already been mentioned; but the screen surpasses it in dimension and in the intricacy of the framework, which is of iron instead of wood, and has its central wings in the shape of an arch. The whole is harmoniously composed, crowned with fleurs-de-lis springing from a double scroll, and completed by a high central finial in the form of a little tree which in turn blossoms with foliage and fleurs-de-lis. This splendid cresting is one of the earliest examples of a floral finial in iron.

The screen in the chapel of the Palazzo Pubblico at Siena (plates 10 and 11) is attributed to Niccolò di Paolo, and was executed in 1436. It consists of a solid framework divided into panels containing nine quatrefoils. On top of the screen is a rich frieze of open-work sheet-iron, lightly embossed with foliage, heraldic shields and, in the centre of the frieze, the Roman wolf feeding Romulus and Remus. Above the screen is a row of spearheads, sprigs of flowers and leaves modelled into vase-shapes, all very well modelled and designed. There is a screen in Sta Trinità, Florence which is very similar in design and structure, and certainly comes from the same Sienese forge. Two very simple screens in

20. Grating. 16th century. Monastery, St Florian.

21. Door. 16th century. Hohensalzburg Fortress, Salzburg.

20.   Grating. 16th century. Monastery, St Florian. This is a classic example of ironwork derived from the decoration of illuminated manuscripts. Most of the bars are circular; they intersect through metal eyelets which have been perforated while hot. The grating is part of the well of the monastery.

21.   Door. 16th century. Hohensalzburg Fortress, Salzburg. Whether or not it is of Northern origin, this door carries motifs derived from the Scandinavian decorative repertoire.

22.   Pomegranate tree in iron. 15th–16th century. Castle of Issogne. Four branches of the tree emit jets of water. This singular work of ironcraft, the only one of its kind, was executed by Pantaleone Lale and Nicolas Longet, the master smiths from the Val d'Aosta, who did a great deal of work for the Counts of Challant.

23.   Gate. 16th century. Villa Barbaro, Masèr (Treviso). Gate in wrought-iron fashioned with flat bands. A floral motif of fluid design, almost calligraphic, is divided into large rectangular panels with a graceful and charming cresting that already foreshadows the Baroque.

22. Pomegranate tree in iron. 15—16th century. Castle of Issogne.

Prato Cathedral must also be mentioned: one, attributed to Giovanni di Cristoforo (1348), in the baptistery; the other, attributed to Bruno di Lapo and Pasquino di Matteo, in the Chapel of the Holy Girdle.

The gate of Orvieto Cathedral is also of Sienese workmanship. It is divided into large panels with quatrefoils, has a frieze with open-work foliage and coats-of-arms, and is surmounted by a cresting of heraldic fleurs-de-lis alternating with long flowering stems. This beautiful work is attributed to the Sienese Jacopo di Lello (1337).

The Sienese craftsmanship of the screen in the Loggia del Bigallo in Florence is charming. The Gothic style has lost some of its Northern severity and acquired a Tuscan lightness and serenity, especially in the arch-shaped fanlight overhead, with quatrefoils radiating downwards in the form of an aureole.

23. Gate. 16th century. Villa Barbaro, Masèr (Treviso).

THE RENAISSANCE

The workshops of Lucca played a similar role during the Renaissance to those of Siena in the Middle Ages. Throughout the 16th and into the 17th century Lucca led and other Italian towns followed. The situation changed only when the exquisite ironwork of the French began to influence Italians.

Luccan workshops produced many fanlights for the doors of palaces in Lucca and other Tuscan towns. Among the most beautiful are the following: Palazzo Boccella, Casa Cenani, Brancoli-Busdraghi, Bonvisi, and Palazzo Orsetti. (The latter is probably earlier, with Gothic reminiscences in its design and execution.)

The smiths of Lucca were anxious to imitate bronze in some of their works. This appears to have happened in some pieces made from blocks of iron, as seems to be the case in the door-knocker of the Palazzo Mazzarosa (17th century), which is all the same a work of great skill and most original in conception.

The 16th-century fanlight of the Monastery of the Brabantines heralds the 17th century in its motifs, enclosed in the spokes of wheels constructed of twisted bars, and in the robust way that the scrolls are made.

The cresset on the Palazzo Baroni, Lucca is contemporary with those made by Caparra for the Palazzo Pitti but so very different in structure and design that it might be taken for 15th-century Gothic. It is a fine example of a work made by flat bands, without any welding or forging: the pieces have been superimposed on each other and then riveted. It looks like the wide calyx of a flower with eight petals, each one terminating in a fleur-de-lis; and charmingly curved lanceolated leaves grow from each petal. The supporting bracket, in the shape of a branch, is also decorated with leaves and a few buds. It is obviously intended to represent a lily stem, a genuine and spontaneous work of popular taste, ingenuously graceful and harmonious.

The lantern on the Palazzo Boccella, Lucca is more of the Renaissance in its structure and design. It is in the form of a shrine, octagonal in plan; on each side there is a little window with an open-work grille in sheet-iron. The windows are surrounded by

24. Bed. 16th century. Casa Bagatti Valsecchi, Milan.

24.   Bed. 16th century. Casa Bagatti Valsecchi, Milan. Bed in wrought-iron, evidently of Sicilian origin. There are numerous examples of this type in the Palermo Museum, an indication of its popularity. The gilded decoration is particularly rich.

25.   Venetian panel. 16th century. Victoria and Albert Museum, London. The mastery of the Venetian smiths is demonstrated here in the forging of this panel. The large four-square bars have been tapered by dexterous blows of the hammer. A characteristic of Venetian ironwork is the joining of the basic elements without riveting or welding.

26.   Grille in a mullioned window. End of the 15th century. Scuola di San Giorgio, Venice. The C-scroll motif is used to obtain a finely proportioned quatrefoil. The fleurs-de-lis, inserted where the scrolls meet, emphasise the charm of the whole.

25. Venetian panel. 16th century. Victoria and Albert
Museum, London.

26. Grille in a mullioned window. End of the 15th century.
Scuola di San Giorgio, Venice.

twisted rods terminating in a pointed arch. The shrine is crowned with a fleur-de-lis. In this example, the supporting bracket also imitates a flowering branch, but the leaves are crenated and have embossed veins, and the buds are opening out. The technique is more advanced than that of the Palazzo Baroni; it is very elegant and finely proportioned.

In northern Italy there was a long tradition of extracting, smelting and forging iron. Whole villages lived by making products of iron: scissors, cutlery, agricultural tools and wood-cutting implements, which Italy exported in great quantities.

In all the northern Italian valleys, colossal water-wheels gave motion and force to the hammers. In the valleys of Brescia, forges have been in operation for over a thousand years, extracting and smelting iron from mines that were already being exploited in Roman times. Equally important are the Val Trompia, the valleys of Bergamo, and Emilia.

Piacenza is rich in ironwork, including the strap-work with foliage decoration on the door of S. Antonino (16th century) and the enormous gate to the main staircase of the Palazzo Farnese (second half of the 16th century). The gate was designed by Vignola and unfortunately, like the magnificent palace itself, was left unfinished. It is surmounted by the ducal crown, and the decoration consists of scrolls in flat iron in continuous movement, following the outline of an asymmetrical design. This creates a field on which the six great lilies of the blazon of the Farnese family are displayed.

Bologna. Some details of the imposing balcony of the Palazzo Bevilacqua (plate 27) recall the door at Palencia and the screen at Lüneberg; but it is far superior to them in design and construction. The large rectangular frontal is divided into eighteen panels, those in the centre broken by a Gothic rose-window of quatrefoil design. Each panel contains four pairs of C-scrolls made of slender twisted bars that terminate in little snakes' heads. The uprights of the framework have also been skilfully forged into a twisted shape, but in three different directions, corresponding to the horizontal bars that complete the supporting frame. The gate (plate 28) and the other parts in wrought-iron are of the same design and manufacture, forged in the workshops of Bologna.

27. Balcony. End of the 15th century. Palazzo Bevilacqua,
Bologna.

28. Gate. End of the 15th century. Palazzo Bevilacqua, Bologna.

29. Cresset. 17th century. Palazzo Saminiati, Lucca.

27.   Balcony. End of the 15th century. Palazzo Bevilacqua, Bologna. Details of this balcony show affinities with the door at Palencia and even with the screen at Lüneburg, but they are inferior to it in imaginativeness and originality of construction.

28.   Gate. End of the 15th century. Palazzo Bevilacqua, Bologna. The decorative motifs of the balcony are found again in this interior gate. Its structure is well-balanced and its proportions harmonious, completely at one with the elegant portico and the overhanging Renaissance loggia.

29.   Cresset. 17th century. Palazzo Saminiati, Lucca. This is a fine work made with flat bands. It was constructed without welding or forging; in other words, the pieces have been superimposed on each other and riveted. It is similar to the better-known cresset on the Palazzo Baroni.

30.   Hinge for a door. 16th–17th century. Victoria and Albert Museum, London. This is a fine example of German craftsmanship of the 16th–17th centuries, an age in which the functional elements were treated as if they were decorative features. In this case, the hinge of the door is in sheet-iron which has been engraved and pierced.

31.   Lock for a casket. 17th century. Victoria and Albert Museum, London. This little masterpiece of German craftsmanship, finely pierced, embossed and engraved, shows how a merely utilitarian object can become the pretext for unrestrained decorative fancy.

30. Hinge for a door. 16th-17th century. Victoria and Albert Museum, London.

31. Lock for a casket. 17th century.
Victoria and Albert Museum, London.

There are several important works in Emilia. The grille of the Casa Chierici has a simple design with bars crossing at right-angles, the transverse bars passing through metal eyelets; in the centre there is a fine fleur-de-lis quatrefoil. There is also the standard-holder at Casa Mari, and another at Casa Magnani, with a spiral bluebell and two small hissing snakes. All these works were certainly of local manufacture.

Venice. Venetian craftsmen were not so skilful in working iron and produced nothing comparable with the famous works of the Florentine, Milanese and Sienese Renaissance. Venetians preferred working in bronze, and obtained many of their iron objects from the towns subject to the Republic, Brescia in particular.

In the 18th century, there was more activity in Venice, prompted by the important building revival in the town and the surrounding districts. Numerous villas were built along the banks of the Brenta; particularly worth seeing are the Villa Zenobia at Sta Bona (near Treviso), the screen with rich cresting in the Villa Pisani at Strà, the Villa Manin at Passariano, and the villa at Grimani. Wrought-ironwork was also used in the interiors of the new buildings for balustrades, gates for staircases, lamps, and such utilitarian objects as braziers, warmers and wash-stands.

Rome. Wrought-ironwork was used in a similar fashion here as in other Italian states, but the most important works were executed during the Baroque period.

Most Renaissance ironwork for architectural features—gates and grilles, for example—were relatively simple in design; for ironworkers were no longer permitted to work on their own initiative but were subject to the architect, who ordered works in iron which he had designed himself.

THE RENAISSANCE OUTSIDE ITALY

The influence of the Italian Renaissance was felt only gradually in the rest of Europe. Craftsmen in iron remained faithful to Gothic forms for quite a long time, especially in Germany and the countries under German influence.

France. French smiths clung to the fashions and forms of the preceding Gothic period for some time. But in certain works the Gothic inheritance was quickly abandoned; for example the screens at Rouen and a very beautiful one at Le Mans with scrolls terminating in palmettes and laurel leaves. The gate in the Musée Carnavalet of Paris is very original; it is constructed with simple square bars with little ornamentation but crowned by a very beautiful cresting decorated with sheaves of ears of corn, wild flowers and agricultural tools (sickles, hoes, rakes and billhooks). It has a fresh and lively pastoral flavour.

Germany. The calligraphic style of German ironwork decoration displays the vitality of the late Gothic imagination. Architects and decorators do not dictate the decorative treatment of a grille; the draughtsmen designers (Dürer, Martin Schongauer) are exclusively responsible. The choir screen in Augsburg Cathedral (plates 18 and 19) is a hallucinatory masterpiece, the design of the larger scrolls generating a maze of whorls that fills the space between the supporting cornices. Most German

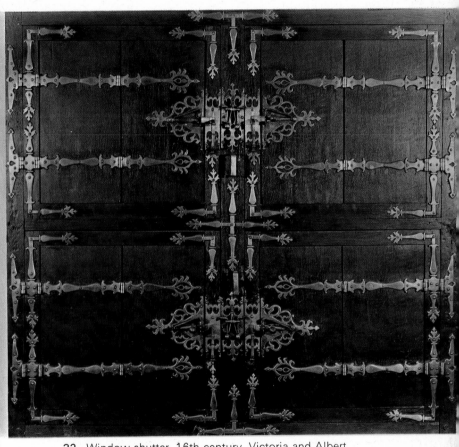

32. Window shutter. 16th century. Victoria and Albert
Museum, London.

32.   Window shutter. 16th century. Victoria and Albert Museum, London. The delicate and graceful decoration follows and emphasises the lines of the wooden surface. The shutter was made in Nuremberg.

33.   Cemetery cross. 17th–18th century. Victoria and Albert Museum, London. This type of polychrome wrought-iron cemetery cross is found throughout Germany and Austria. Its structure is obscured by the exuberant decorative tracery.

34.   Key plate. 17th century. Victoria and Albert Museum, London. This is an example of Spanish craftsmanship, finely pierced and engraved. The rhythm of the tree motif, with figures apparently growing from it, is oddly Art Nouveau in feeling.

33. Cemetery cross. 17th–18th century. Victoria and Albert Museum, London.

34. Key plate. 17th century. Victoria and Albert Museum, London.

ironwork from Late Gothic to Renaissance is based on a calligraphic style, even when the decoration is not directly inspired by manuscript illuminations. The railings that surround the tomb of Maximilian in the Imperial Church at Innsbruck, for example, date from the second half of the 16th century; yet the decoration still consists of round bars bent in figures-of-eight which are repeated inside each other numerous times, forming a web around the intersections where the bars cross. This is a motif with many variants, for example, the protective grating of the well at the Castle of Grafenegg in Austria, dated 1570, and another grating in the Church of St Ulrich in Augsburg, dated 1580. In the same church, there is an example which has been completely simplified in the lower section; this consists of simple cylindrical bars with a few collars and rings, but surmounted by a beautiful cresting in the form of small arches, and decorated inside with C-scrolls without excessive interweaving. In the middle of the 17th century, there was a return to single and double figure-of-eight motifs interweaving with each other in the church of St Peter at Görlitz, near Dresden; also revived there were scrolls terminating in palmettes, magnolias and fleurs-de-lis with spiral- and cone-shaped buds, or even little heads of grotesques.

In a chapel of a church at Breslau, there is a late 17th-century gate decorated with corn-cobs made of slender twisted cast-iron rods. A singular large flower imitating a passion-flower rises from the central bar of the gate between two flowering finials. The small cylindrical chapel on the parapet surrounding the well at Neisse (Silesia) is a masterpiece of German wrought-iron work. It is enclosed by large flat bands which are finely engraved; they are divided into three sections with different designs. The chapel is crowned with a cupola. The decoration is partly comprised of scrolls of round iron, partly of flat bars variously worked with grotesques, palmettes and other elements taken from the graphic repertoire of Irish illuminated manuscripts. The entire work is engraved by punching.

Many 16th- and 17th-century German works of wrought-iron are strongly described as Renaissance in style. The new style presupposed greater clarity of line and texture of ironwork. This was not always grasped in Germany and France—or in Spain, where a decorative impulse inherited from the Moors encouraged smiths to fill every available space.

In general, however, Spanish grilles acquired an appearance of greater clarity although their decorative details remained exuberant. Examples include the splendid screens in Barcelona Cathedral, and those of the cathedrals of Seville (1530), Plasencia in Estremadura, Saragossa and Jerez. The magnificent screen of the Royal Chapel in Granada Cathedral (plate 15) is divided into three architectural orders and supported by classical-style columns and twisted vertical bars. Between two columns in the centre of the second order is a large trophy consisting of an eagle crowned with laurel wreaths, and figures and foliage. Along the top of the screen runs a cresting of eleven candlesticks, their upper halves linked by a design of scrolls, berries and acanthus leaves; framed by the candlesticks and the top bar of the screen are ten scenes from the life of Jesus, embossed and engraved on sheet-iron. Towering above all, in the centre, is a large crucifix in high relief.

The screen at Jerez de la Frontera in Andalusia, dates back to the 16th century but is of a Baroque exuberance. It is not as large as the screen at Granada, but just as richly decorated. The iron is partly embossed and partly pierced, so that it appears to be in high relief.

The two shutters of a 16th-century palace at Salamanca display Gothic elements as developed in Spain. One consists of three curved parts, little shrines lying adjacent to each other and terminating in a pointed cupola; the other, also divided into three, has three little windows with imitation Gothic arches flowering with vine leaves. Each shutter has a grille of vertical bars made by twisted rods alternating with straight hexagonal rods. The grilles make an austere, Moorish impression, though it has been toned down with horizontal friezes of pierced sheet-iron with foliage and Latin sayings. Convex shells of undoubted heraldic significance are prominently placed at various points on both grilles.

The 16th-century gates in Palencia Cathedral and in the University of Salamanca, display the predominant motifs of Spanish ironwork. On their

35. Lock. 17th century. Victoria and Albert
Museum. London.

35.   Lock. 17th century. Victoria and Albert Museum, London. In this Spanish lock, the techniques used in making it—the engraving of the key plate, the pierced work of the decoration —achieve a fine effect of balance.

36.   Tabernacle door. 17th century. Victoria and Albert Museum, London. Attributed to Lombard smiths on account of its style and working. In order to make works of this kind it was necessary to use sheet-iron, which permitted the introduction of the new decorative elements characteristic of the Baroque— here, acanthus leaves rich in curves and flowers.

37.   Screen in the Chapel of the Saints of the Annunciation. 17th century. Church of Sta Maria sopra Minerva, Rome. A composite work on which various techniques have been used. It is constructed of square and flat bars and rods. A beautiful piece of ironwork which achieves extremely original effects.

36. Tabernacle door. 17th century. Victoria and Albert Museum, London.

37. Screen in the Chapel of the Saints of the Annunciation.
17th century. Church of Sta Maria sopra Minerva, Rome.

principal axis the vertical bars are formed by rods on which architectural motifs have been applied: small bases and capitals at the extremities, and a central spindle-shaped shaft; they look as if they have been made by a technique of turning and casting rather than by using the hammer. The gate at Palencia is inserted into a pointed arch, its cresting following the curve of the arch; the gate at Salamanca is rectangular. Renaissance elements have been applied on both.

BAROQUE AND ROCOCO

Technical progress enabled the 17th-century artist to exploit the malleability of iron in astonishing ways. His fancy was no longer restrained; he could indulge in the strangest curves and most luxuriant foliage, secure in the knowledge that anything and everything could be done. Wrought-ironwork thus emulates the extravagances of the other Baroque arts.

In the 17th century, France regained the leadership of the arts, and held it for most of the 18th century. The styles of Louis XIV, XV and XVI were of the highest standard of elegance. In ironwork this entailed forcing the metal into daring curves and flourishes. A new way of working was developed, richer and more vivacious in the construction and ornamentation of gates, parapets, balconies, grilles and staircases; and it employed the same motifs as other Baroque and Rococo materials—cornices, crestings, coats-of-arms, cartouches, etc. The construction of great ornamental screens—for example, those at Versailles, at the botanical gardens of Angers, at the castle at Dampierre in the Aube, at Bagatelle, the Archiepiscopal Palace at Sens, and so forth—must be passed over in order to discuss Lamour's masterpiece for the Place Stanislas at Nancy. The Place Stanislas was built according to the plans of the architect Héré, and constitutes one of the most striking of all urban complexes. This is largely due to the work of Lamour, the smith at the court of King Stanislas, who made the palaces surrounding the square stand out in greater relief with imposing railings in black and gold.

The square influenced European ironwork for a century. Only the Germans rivalled the French

38. Crucifix screen (central part). 17th century. Lucerne Cathedral.

38. Crucifix screen (central part). 17th century. Lucerne Cathedral. Extremely beautiful, even if it is not as imposing as the one at Einsiedeln. Also notable are the screens at St Ulrich in Augsburg, Constance Cathedral and the Clementine College at Prague.

39. Right-hand gate of the crucifix screen. 17th century. Lucerne Cathedral. Several screens with this type of suggested perspective design are found in Germany, Australia, Poland and Switzerland. In the detail that is reproduced here the design is in relief.

40. Balcony railing. 18th century. Victoria and Albert Museum, London. From Versailles; embossed sheet-iron. The rocaille decorative motifs have not been completely assimilated; in fact the work has a certain Baroque heaviness.

39. Right-hand gate of the crucifix screen. 17th century. Lucerne Cathedral.

40. Balcony railing. 18th century. Victoria and Albert Museum, London.

work. The railings surrounding the courtyard of Würzburg Castle form a line broken many times at the corner and then shaped to a curve, creating a superb design of floral motifs around the courtyard.

French wrought-ironwork was of greater grace, even if executed with less technical virtuosity. The castle at Dampierre in the Aube (Basse Champagne) has gates typical of the transitional period at the beginning of the 18th century, with a beautiful cresting decorated with coats-of-arms, monograms and laurel wreaths. Even richer in rocaille decorations, and with a rich flowering finial, is the gate in the castle of Bagatelle.

There is a wonderful screen, dated 1730, at Sens in the Orleans district. It has a cresting on to which is bound a cardinal's coat-of-arms encircled by palm and acanthus leaves. A work of great importance and high artistic value is the screen in Nancy Cathedral (plate 42), dating from the middle of the 18th century; it has been attributed to Lamour or his school. One of the major masterpieces of the art of ironwork is also at Nancy and by Lamour: the incomparable staircase in the Town Hall (plate 41).

There are two railings at Paris dating from the second half of the 18th century: one surrounding the Palace of the Military School, and the other the Law Courts. They are attributed to the same workshop and were also certainly designed by the same man. The style is very restrained and austere, a prelude to Neo-Classicism. The large crestings are executed in masterly fashion and support dominating decorative motifs: a crescent-shaped shield upheld by laurel and oak wreaths; and a coat-of-arms with the three lilies of France, surrounded by palm leaves and festoons, and surmounted by the royal crown.

At the beginning of the Baroque period, most German and Austrian wrought-ironwork still contained vigorous Gothic elements; only in the 18th century was work inspired by the new style produced. An obvious example of the gradual assimilation of the new motifs is the screen in the Church of St Emmeran at Ratisbon: at the top of the Gothic framework is a cresting that is clearly Baroque. The screen in the Church of St Ulrich at Augsburg (plate 49) presents the same anomaly, whereas the

41. Main staircase. 18th century. Town Hall, Nancy.

42. Screen of the main chapel. 18th century. Nancy
Cathedral.

41. Main staircase. 18th century. Town Hall, Nancy. Jean Lamour, smith to the court of King Stanislas, made this staircase balustrade from the design of the architect Héré; it is an incomparable masterpiece of ironwork, dating from about 1755. Lamour also made the famous balustrade in the Place Stanislas at Nancy.

42. Screen of the main chapel. 18th century. Nancy Cathedral. This is in pure Louis XV style, in black and gilt. It is from the forge of Jean Lamour, and dates from about 1750, the period when rocaille art reached its apogee.

43. Staircase balustrade. 18th century. Hôtel de Marcilly, Paris. A work of exquisite design and masterly construction, with square and flat bars and some gilding; dated about 1700.

44. Staircase balustrade. 18th century. Compiègne Castle, France. Elegant wrought-ironwork with medallions and crowns of foliage in embossed and gilded sheet-iron; from about the second half of the 18th century. The design displays classical tendencies.

43. Staircase. 18th century. Hôtel de Marcilly, Paris.

44. Staircase. 18th century. Compiègne Castle, France.

screen in the Church of the Holy Cross, also in Augsburg, is definitely in the new style.

The screen in Graz Cathedral (Austria) and the magnificent gates of the Palace of Belvedere in Vienna display a high standard of technical skill and exquisite decorative taste; particularly noteworthy is the central gate to the Palace itself. The screen in the Franciscan church at Salzburg is a festive composition of delicate construction, clearly executed by the hand of a master.

The technical excellence of smiths throughout the Austrian Empire offers a variety of artistic interpretations—how varied can be seen by comparing the two gates of the Clementine College at Prague, which obviously show Italian influence, with others in the Church of St Salvador in the same town and of the same period. And also in museums in Nuremberg and Munich there are ornaments of great interest in forged iron, embossed work and chasing. They appear to be fragments of screens or examples of decorative work for purposes of demonstration; and they are indeed instructive because they allow us to comprehend the new method of working necessary for Baroque and Rococo decoration. In addition to the cylindrical or polygonal bars which had sufficed during the Gothic and Renaissance periods, it had now become necessary to use sheet-iron, which permitted the execution of the decorative motifs peculiar to the Baroque style: acanthus leaves with elaborate curves and cartouches, curly sea-lettuces with fringes, and the whole abstract repertoire of fantastic Rococo flora. The smith was obliged to add new, often unusual tools to the traditional implements of the forge, for example various chisels—cross-cut, half-moon shaped, olive-shaped, etc. All this brought about a real technical revolution.

Thus ironwork, which for centuries had been restricted to decoration on flat surfaces, entered the third dimension. It became possible to create the masterpieces in iron which were supreme expressions of a style and of an epoch: the railings of the Place Stanislas at Nancy and of Würzburg Castle, both executed towards the middle of the 18th century.

The two works differ in structural conception and decorative inspiration. The French work is composed within a geometrical framework and is more classical, with pointed or depressed entrance arches, with a wide straight terminal cornice strongly moulded like a real entablature. The finials and decoration is composed of foliage, rocaille rosettes, superimposed or placed externally on the pilasters or columns themselves. The decoration is delineated by square bars with a prevalence of vertical lines interrupted by mixtilinear lines which unfold with a refined elegance in rigidly symmetrical motifs. The decoration is composed of foliage, 'rocaille' rosettes, flamboyant flourishes, lambrequins, small shields in sheet-iron embossed, engraved or pierced, and joined to the bars of the structure. The gilding with which Lamour covered the embossed ornaments emphasises the preciosity and masterly technique of its execution.

The screen at Würzburg also retains ascending square bars for the main structure; but the cornices of the cresting, which is very thick and simply moulded, have a strongly mixtilinear movement, that gave great decorative freedom to the plastic imagination of the creator. The quality which in the French work displayed itself in elegance, restrained freedom and decorative moderation, in the German gate exploded into incredible ironwork vegetation which was daringly executed in three dimensions with sparse symmetrical motifs.

There were many other notable examples of wrought-ironwork in the rich and fertile Baroque period. France, Germany, Austria, Hungary, Denmark, Switzerland, England, Spain, Italy were all active to a greater or lesser extent. To take only the example of Switzerland: at Basle there are railings of exquisite design which surround palaces and 18th-century villas; at Zürich there are some fine Rococo railings; and the Collegiate church at St Gall is dominated by the imposing choir screen made in 1770.

ITALY IN THE 17TH AND 18TH CENTURIES

In the second half of the 17th century, Baroque architectural works that influenced the whole of the civilised world were produced in Italy. Nevertheless, the use of ironwork in conjunction with architecture was for a long time limited to entrance gates, doors or dividing screens in churches. It was of an extremely austere line, with a prevalence of vertical square bars broken by a few mixtilinear bars and occasionally crowned with crestings that were almost always decorated with fleur-de-lis spearheads.

There are many Roman screens from the first Baroque period. A good example is the exterior screen in St John Lateran, which is surmounted by a beautiful cresting with a papal coat-of-arms inserted in it. Other screens with crestings are in S. Pietro in Vincoli; the portico of S. Maria delle Grazie; and the portico of St John Lateran, whose structure displays the movement and mixtilinear cresting of late Baroque.

In Rome itself, as elsewhere in Italy, Baroque architects preferred marble and stone for balustrades, stair railings and balconies. But iron railings, balconies and grilles appear in a number of villas around Rome, particularly in the Frascati district; for example the villas Aldobrandini, Borghese, Lancellotti, Falconieri, Torlonia.

45. Balcony railing. 18th century. Victoria and Albert Museum, London.

45. Balcony railing. 18th century. Victoria and Albert Museum, London. From Lorraine; it dates from about 1750. This charming rocaille work demonstrates the great technical skill of French smiths in working wrought-iron, allowing them to create the most capricious and unpredictable movements.

46. Interior screen. 18th century. Church of St-Roch, Paris. The structure, restrained lines and relative decorative sobriety of this piece anticipate the Neo-Classical style.

47. Communion rail. 18th century. Church of St-Roch, Paris. The transition from the rocaille repoussé style to the Louis XVI classicism is expressed here in the lively relief work of flowers and acanthus leaves in gilded sheet-iron.

46. Interior screen. 18th century. Church of St-Roch, Paris.

47. Communion rail. 18th century. Church of St-Roch, Paris.

The Venetian *barocchetto*, a delightful variant of the Baroque, made a lively contribution to ironwork. Examples are the splendid gate in the Palazzo Pisani with rocaille work in sheet-iron; the gate in the Villa Reale at Strà, with richly crowned cresting; the gates of the Church of Tramonte in the Euganean hills; and the gate in the Palazzo Capodilista at Padua.

The many palaces and other important buildings of Genoa contain numerous examples of 17th-century ironwork, which is also found in the surrounding countryside, as in the grille of the Palazzo Picedi-Groppallo at Sarzana, with its rich flowering rocaille cresting.

Little ironwork is used on the Baroque masterpieces of Filippo Juvarra at Turin. Three superb door screens at the Palazzo Madama deserve to be mentioned. They decorate the three entrance arches to the large atrium, and are of a rigorous structure, formed of square bars and vertical straps running the whole length of the wings. They are divided into three horizontal bands with dense geometrical motifs containing the heraldic symbols of the Cross of Savoy and the fleur-de-lis of France. A similar decorative principle has been used for the arch of the fanlight; a central circle encloses the inter-twined monogram of Madama Reale Maria Cristina. The grilles on the ground floor are beautiful but austere in design.

Around Novara there are many screens, grilles and gratings of local manufacture. The screen in a chapel of Sacro Monte at Orta is an extremely beautiful example of primitive Baroque, with decorative scrolls in slender straps bound in bundles and then tied with ribbons to resemble cross-bows. The partly-curved, partly-straight lines and corkscrew tendrils of the Baroque have been adopted, and the screen is crowned with a finial of lilies in thin sheet-iron.

At Varallo Sesia there is an interesting series of small but graceful balconies of good Rococo design, with rocailles worked and embossed in sheet-iron.

There is a good deal of important ironwork in Lombardy. An amazing work, forged by Carlo Cotturi in 1737, is the great screen in the Ossuary of Cepina in the province of Sondrio. It was constructed of flat bars discreetly twisted and entwined, or

48. Screen. Beginning of the 18th century. Graz Cathedral.

48.   Screen. Beginning of the 18th century. Graz Cathedral. A work of delicate design and graceful execution. Its elegant and light structure belongs to the spirit of early Rococo. Like the magnificent gates of the Belvedere Palace at Vienna, it is technically superb.

49.   Screen. 18th century. Church of St Ulrich, Augsburg. A rich screen with strong architectural structures and sumptuous, beautifully made crestings. It is also important because of the perspective devices used on it.

50.   Detail of railings. 18th century. Castle park, Würzburg. This is the masterpiece of German Baroque ironcraft; a decorative composition of incomparable boldness, executed with unequalled technical skill. The use of vigorous reliefs in sheet-iron creates an impressive three-dimensional effect.

51.   Main gate. 18th century. Castle park, Würzburg. From the workshop which created the work in the previous plate; it is crowned by a rich cresting with the regal coat-of-arms. The elaborate, almost overpowering iron vegetation stands out three-dimensionally; it flowers and shoots forth unpredictably, but always with supreme harmony.

49. Screen. 18th century. Church of St Ulrich, Augsburg.

50. Detail of railings. 18th century. Castle park, Würzburg.

51. Main gate. 18th century. Castle park, Würzburg.

fashioned with fleurs-de-lis or trefoil motifs; the whole is attached to a framework of a few close-knit and well-fitting divisions with three large magnificent fanlights overhead.

In the museum of the Castello Sforzesco in Milan, there is a grille or parlour grating. It is constructed with square bars and straps in a technique similar to that used for the screen at Orta. There is a charming balustrade (plate 53) of more advanced technique in the Museo Poldi Pezzoli; it encircles a highly elaborate marble Rococo fountain.

Emilian workshops continued to produce elegant, technically perfect work during the 17th century, whereas Venetian, Piedmont and Lombardian forges gradually succumbed to French influence. A smith who rivalled and perhaps surpassed the elegance of French work was Giobatta Malagoli (1729–1797) of Modena, who was famous and honoured throughout Europe. His ironwork is hammered with softness and dexterity; and although he of course worked to designs made by architects and designers, the sensitivity with which he translated them into metal makes them separate works of art in their own right.

Malagoli executed many important works at Modena, especially in the hospital (1753–1758). In the entrance hall he placed iron gratings, overthrows, fanlights and charming gates. He also worked in the University, and in various private palaces such as Montellari and Sabatini. The influence of his workshop can undoubtedly be seen in other Emilian villages, and in towns on the borders of lower Lombardy.

The fine gate in S. Sisto at Piacenza was made in a local forge at about the beginning of the 18th century. It carries dense decorated scrolls which spring from wide branches with graceful curves; they are tied to the centre in a symmetrical pattern by twisted metal laces and cords. The gate is enclosed by an arched portal; in a rectangular partition under the fanlight there is a design of decorated scrolls in the shape of a large butterfly. Such a beautiful and original design must have been conceived by an artistic imagination of the first order. Also very beautiful, and from the same workshop are the gate in the entrance hall of Casa Zanardi at Cremona, the gate of the Civic Museum at Piacenza (1717), the little gate of Palazzo Costa, and some balcony railings in Piacenza.

Acireale in Sicily possesses the superb church of S. Sebastiano, which was completed in 1705 after the earthquake of the preceding century; around the church arose a new town, mainly in a very beautiful Baroque style. The church itself contains five beautiful exterior screens with rich crestings by the hand of a master, and in the town there are very many parapet railings, iron galleries and balconies of the most exquisite Sicilian *barocchetto*. The first floor of the Town Hall, which is surrounded by small iron balconies, is a notable piece of work; so are the entrance gates to the Chapel of the Blessed Sacrament in Syracuse Cathedral, which form a lace-like pattern. The portal and the two side doors of the cathedral are adorned with wrought-iron screens in a vivacious Sicilian Baroque style. Ragusa Cathedral is one of the most successful expressions of Sicilian Baroque, with a magnificent screen around the monumental entrance staircase.

Ironwork is rare in the large sacred or secular buildings of the main towns, but common in private Baroque palaces and houses. The pleasant Palazzo Biscari at Catania, for example, boasts a graceful

52. Detail of the main gate. 18th century. Castle park,
Würzburg.

52.   Detail of the main gate. 18th century. Castle park, Würzburg. Germans kept a taste for the Baroque long after the decline of the style in France and Italy. Its fantastic splendour was almost exclusively sustained by an astonishing technical skill.

53.   Staircase in the entrance hall. 18th century. Museo Poldi Pezzoli, Milan. The pleasingly designed balustrade with large flowing volutes in flat iron bars is an exquisite work of Lombard manufacture. The metal straps are held firm by links without welding. This charming gilded piece is a splendid frame for the graceful little Rococo fountain in white marble.

54.   Entrance gate to the Corsini Chapel. 18th century. Basilica of St John Lateran, Rome. The structure and decoration already bear the imprint of Neo-Classicism. The technique is nearer to casting than to the traditional method of iron-working by hammer. The gilding of the whole confirms this impression.

55.   Grille. Beginning of the 18th century. Church of Sta Maria Novella, Florence. The grille is in four-square wrought-iron. The design is of the transitional period between Renaissance and Baroque. The symmetrical motifs of the composition blend pleasingly into the Gothic mullioned window of the Spanish chapel.

53. Staircase in the entrance hall. 18th century. Museo Poldi Pezzoli, Milan.

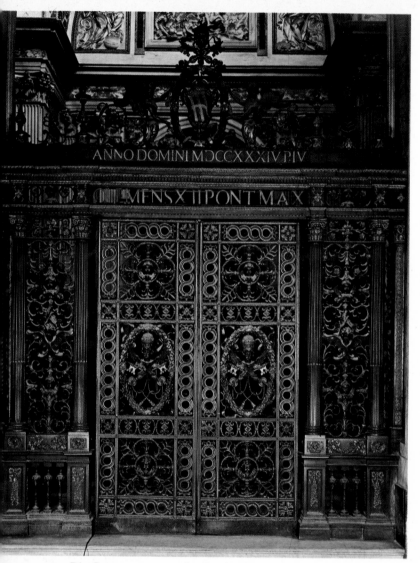

54. Entrance gate to the Corsini Chapel. 18th century.
Basilica of St John Lateran, Rome.

55. Grille. Beginning of the 18th century. Church of Sta Maria Novella, Florence.

interior staircase with an iron balustrade of exquisite Rococo design. Railings and balconies were popular in Catania, as elsewhere in Sicily.

Catanian ironwork is Baroque in style, with decorated scrolls and palmettes, vanes, spearheads, halberds and the little heads of plumed paladins; whereas Palermo work retains strong Moorish elements, being constructed of rods forged in various S-shapes and then flattened out so as to form small lenticular discs. The severe line of this ironwork was then enlivened by colour, and the little discs were transformed into little flowers.

THE ENGLISH REVIVAL

England also experienced a revival under the impact of Continental developments. During the Middle Ages two masterpieces of the first importance had been produced: Thomas de Leghtone's great Eleanor Grille at Westminster Abbey, constructed in 1294 to protect the tomb of Edward I's queen, Eleanor of Castile; and John Tresilian's splendidly intricate gates and screen for Edward IV's chantry in St George's Chapel, Windsor Castle. But 16th- and 17th-century production was competent but unimaginative blacksmiths' work, with few pretensions to aesthetic achievement—a situation changed only by the arrival of Jean Tijou.

Tijou was a French Huguenot, and quite possibly came to England in the train of William of Orange and Mary. He is easily the most important figure in modern English wrought-ironwork, both in terms of his achievements and his influence on English smiths. It was he who introduced into England the elaborate decorative style of French work, with its embossing and lavish interlacing and leafwork, the best known example being the screen of the Fountain Garden at Hampton Court, which Tijou covered with a mass of acanthus leaves, heraldic emblems and masks. His work for Sir Christopher Wren at St Paul's Cathedral is somewhat more restrained, almost certainly reflecting Wren's more sober taste.

Even more effective in disseminating the new style was the *New Booke of Drawings Invented and Desined by John Tijou* (1693), which contained the original designs for Tijou's English works, as well as many designs inspired by such contemporary French court designers as Marot, Lepautre and Berain. As a result, Tijou's style became known even in the provinces, and imitations of it can be found in most parts of the country.

None of Tijou's English successors was quite his equal, and few produced work of such decorative exuberance; though perhaps the most important, Robert Bakewell of Derby, created an exotic and spectacular garden arbour at Melbourne Hall near Derby (1708–1711). Bakewell's other works, notably the chancel screen and gates in Derby Cathedral (1722–1725), are more restrained.

Closest to Tijou and Continental styles were two Welsh smiths, the Davies brothers, who made the amazing Baroque gates of Chirk Castle near Llangollen. This, like Bakewell's garden arbour, was an early work, and of a decorative complexity never again attempted by its creators; which suggests that the extravagant enthusiasm generated by Tijou was soon replaced (whether in the smiths or their patrons) by more temperate attitudes.

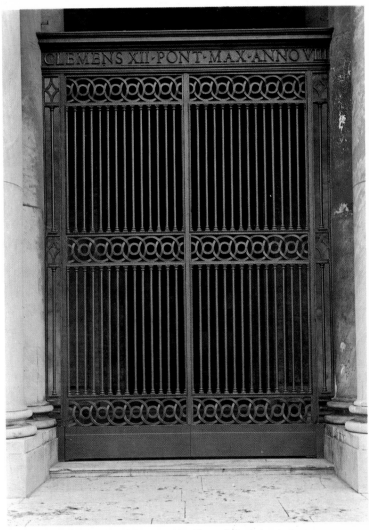

56. Exterior gate. 18th century. Basilica of St John Lateran, Rome.

57. Balcony balustrade. 18th century. Victoria and Albert
Museum, London.

58. Balcony balustrade. 18th century. Victoria and Albert
Museum, London.

56.   Exterior gate. 18th century. Basilica of St John Lateran, Rome. This simple, noble piece of ironwork from a Roman workshop was certainly constructed in the first half of the 18th century. Its severe structure and motifs anticipate the Neo-Classical style.

57.   Balcony balustrade. 18th century. Victoria and Albert Museum, London. Wrought-ironwork with gilded brass ornaments. The sobriety of its composition and the linearity of its decoration are clearly Neo-Classical. It dates from about the end of the 18th century.

58.   Balcony balustrade. 18th century. Victoria and Albert Museum, London. The embossed ornaments in sheet-iron or cast-lead herald the adoption of elements obtained by smelting in cast-iron or brass; these were used from the end of the 18th century.

59.   Upper part of a gate. First half of the 18th century. Victoria and Albert Museum, London. The gate, constructed of square bars and slender straps, with decoration in turned brass. is a fine example of English iron craftsmanship. The ornamental elements are sober and light, typical of the taste of the period.

59. Upper part of a gate. First half of the 18th century. Victoria and Albert Museum, London.

The Davies brothers carried out several other commissions that deserve to be mentioned, for example the 'white' and 'black' gates of Leeswood Hall (Mold, Flintshire), and those of the parish churches at Wrexham and Oswestry. Also important were William Edney (the gates of St Mary Redcliffe, Bristol), Thomas Robinson (gate and screen of the garden at New College, Oxford), and Warren, Buncker and the Paris family. Robinson exemplified the English tendency to abandon the embossed work favoured by Tijou, the disadvantage of which was a tendency to obscure the supple lines of the iron body; in his gate for New College Robinson created a work with splendid linear rhythms, in which a complex effect is achieved with no sacrifice of clarity.

The great age of English ironwork lasted only a few decades. After about 1750 smiths were increasingly constrained to follow the stereotyped designs provided by architects, while the demand for ironwork decreased as the formal garden encased in iron gave way to the 'natural' landscaped garden popularised by Capability Brown and Humphry Repton.

In England, as elsewhere, the smith's craft declined with the Industrial Revolution, and wrought-iron-work of any quality was produced only after the beginning of the Gothic Revival in the 19th century.

NEO-CLASSICISM

Neo-Classicism constricted ironwork into purely graphic designs, conceding nothing to the plasticity of hammered iron. True, Neo-Classical motifs include palmettes, rosettes, bosses and little stars; but they are superimposed or attached rather than integrated creatively into the design.

The making of such ornaments is nearer to the craft of casting than the more overtly creative art of the smith. The main geometrical scheme incorporates such elements as trellis-work, concentric rings joined to each other with aureoles, flights of little arches, and small circles, side by side or overlapping, between parallel lines; there are also diamond-shapes, segments of intersecting circles, tangents, ovals and ellipses. The whole is constructed with bars or straps at sharp angles, polished, perfect and seemingly without welding between the decorative elements and the bars or frame. Instead there are screws, invisible rivets, joins made by moulded collars or with twisted and gilded metal cords, swaged or cast rosettes, and bosses. Other elements are not geometrical but are very stylised, and form part of the decorative repertoire of the whole Neo-Classical period: spearheads with or without fringes, quivers, arrows, crossbows, shields, panoplies, harps, garlands, festoons, and so on.

Neo-Classical ironwork could scarcely have been different. The craftsman had to obey the designer's plans absolutely; interpretation was clearly impossible within a scheme of ice-like geometry. The purity of the forms and neatness of the details compelled smiths to experiment with new methods of working that entailed a complete transformation of their equipment.

The transition from Baroque and Rococo to Neo-Classicism was of course gradual, and varied in speed from place to place: we come across works in the late Baroque period which are already classical in style, and Baroque works made when Neo-Classicism is in full swing. Two examples of these different tendencies are the balustrades of the staircases of the Trianon (Versailles) and the Castle of Compiègne (plate 44) and the two Persian railings surrounding the Military School and the Law Courts.

Neo-Classical wrought-ironwork is less common in the 19th century, since architects usually preferred to use marble. Balconies and outside staircases are rare, but there are some interior balustrades. Screens are very simple, usually constructed of rods with lances and halberds, with a few essential motifs on the horizontal linking bars. Everywhere bronze and cast-iron were becoming popular. A few fanlights in wrought-iron were still produced, as well as hall lanterns and grilles, but light-fittings, lamp-brackets and table-lamps were forged in bronze or brass; at best there was some complementary foliage in sheet-iron.

For over half of the 19th century, the craft of ironwork was in decay. Much of the art of the period consisted of second-rate adaptions of the styles of the past. Flowers and leaves were screw-punched or

60. Gate. 19th century. Villa Pallavicini Trivulzio, S. Fiorano.

60.   Gate. 19th century. Villa Pallavicini Trivulzio, S. Fiorano. Main gate of strict Neo-Classical design; its decorative details were executed with iron straps. The rosettes and medallions are in cast brass. The work dates from 1842, and is part of a purely graphic scheme which concedes nothing to the plasticity of the material.

61.   Balconies of the Casa Ferrario in the Via Spadari. 1902–1905. Milan. The work of the architect Ernesto Pirovano, and a classic example of Italian floral architecture. The wrought-iron balconies are extremely well-constructed and pleasing in design. After the stagnation of the Neo-Classical period, the resumption of working in the traditional manner, with the hammer, was revived in France by Viollet-le-Duc and also made rapid progress in Italy.

62.   Antonio Gaudí. Güell Palace. 1885–1889. Barcelona. One of the many original architectural works of the celebrated Spanish architect Antonio Gaudí; it displays a curious mixture of Gothic and Moorish influences. In the characteristic parabolic arches of this construction Gaudí has inserted grilles rather than gates, in a densely-knit 'Moorish' geometrical design. The gates carry fanlights in strong relief with a remarkable, bizarre serpentine design.

61. Balconies of the Casa Ferrario in the Via Spadari.
1902–1905. Milan.

62. Antonio Gaudí. Güell Palace. 1885—1889. Barcelona.

63. Alessandro Mazzucotelli. Vase with a tree. 19th–20th century. Villa Maria Luisa, Milan.

64. Alessandro Mazzucotelli. Rose window. 19th–20th century. Villa Maria Luisa, Milan.

63.   Alessandro Mazzucotelli. Vase with a tree. 19th–20th century. Villa Maria Luisa, Milan. The little tree carries a wrought-iron garden lamp-holder. The work reveals a delicate and original taste, and represents an attempt to break with the floral style of Art Nouveau.

64.   Alessandro Mazzucotelli. Rose window. 19th–20th century. Villa Maria Luisa, Milan. Rose window like a stylised planet with a flaming aureole. This too demonstrates Mazzucotelli's lively and original imagination.

65.   Flight of steps to a small staircase. 19th–20th century. Villa Maria Luisa, Milan. A superb example of forging solid bars and using sheet-iron of great thickness. The modelling of the large knots is very much in the style of Alessandro Mazzucotelli.

66.   Restaurant sign. 1936–1937. Scuole Professionali della Società Umanitaria, Milan. The sign is in large sheet-iron embossed with rocaille designs; it was executed in the department of metalwork after a design by Umberto Zimelli.

65. Flight of steps to a small staircase. 19th—20th century. Villa Maria Luisa, Milan.

66. Restaurant sign. 1936–1937. Scuole Professionali della
Società Umanitaria, Milan.

mechanically stamped; and the hundreds of cast-iron forgings for grilles, balconies and ramps were nothing more than prefabricated pieces which could be used on any kind of building.

THE REVIVAL OF IRONWORK

In the middle of the 19th century, the French architect Viollet-le-Duc revived the traditional working of wrought-iron in his workshops at Chapelle St Denis. The smith's activity remained limited, however, to work for a few builders of luxurious and aristocratic residences; to make a living most workers had to produce objects intended for the interiors of houses — utilitarian objects or pieces to complement the furnishings. Ironwork was assimilated to the various 19th-century styles, including Art Nouveau with its capricious flourishes, Gallée being prompted by his botanical researches to force iron into forms alien to the nature of the material.

The revival nonetheless spread rapidly throughout

Europe, and at the Paris Exhibition of 1889 German wrought-iron rivalled the works of more experienced French artists. It was at the exhibition that the achievement of Emile Robert, who had restored the craft of ironwork in France, was given European recognition. Robert profited from his friendship with such famous contemporary architects as Magne, Credamme, Pradelle and Plumet, with whom he collaborated in interpreting their designs. His school had many proselytes who in turn became famous: Brandt, Szabó, the Nics brothers, the Capon brothers, Louis Majorelle. The French revival deeply influenced Belgium, where numerous workshops came into being under the guidance of such masters as Lefêbre, Jaspar, Alexandre, Edmond, Paul and Pierre Lacoste.

Italy remained behind for some years, but gradually produced outstanding masters in charge of workshops in various parts of the country. At the first International Exhibition of Decorative Art (Monza, 1923) the superiority of Italian wrought-iron over that of all other countries was recognised; and it was confirmed at the Exhibitions of Paris and Monza

(1925). The leading masters were Alessandro Mazzucotelli, Carlo Rizzarda, Umberto Bellotto, Alberto
Gerardi, Alberto Calligaris, and the brothers Matteuci
of Faenza.

Alessandro Mazzucotelli was the founder of the
Monza Higher Institute of Decorative Arts (1922–
1939), which was particularly celebrated for the
wrought-iron works made by its students. Giorgio
Nicodemi describes his style: 'Mazzucotelli . . . had a
passion for his material . . . Mazzucotelli's inventions,
harmonious and slender, reveal a delicate imagination which always keeps to exact proportions.' He
declared that iron must remain iron, and should be
worked by fire and hammer, which alone gave
authenticity to the work of the smith.

Carlo Rizzarda was the first of Mazzucotelli's
pupils to become famous. He was praised by Papini
as 'an artist capable of dominating the material which
he had chosen'. He also points out that Rizzarda had
learnt from Mazzucotelli the subtle art of beating iron
to preserve its harshness and the vivid imprint of
the hammer.

The Venetian Umberto Bellotto had a sensational

67. Lobster. 1936. Higher
Institute for the Artistic
Industries, Monza.

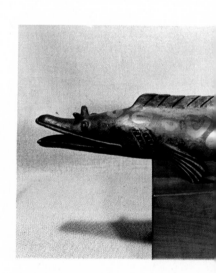

68. Moray eel. 1936. Higher
Institute for the Artistic
Industries, Monza.

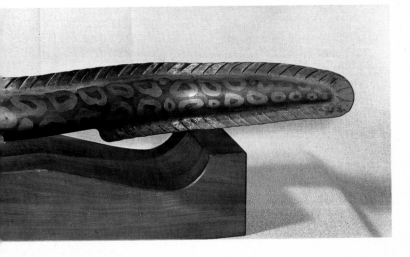

67.   Lobster. 1936. Higher Institute for the Artistic Industries, Monza. A large lobster with its body embossed in thick sheet-iron, but with pincers and claws forged in solid iron. This work was executed by Luigi Cappello, a student at the Institute.

68.   Moray eel. 1936. Higher Institute for the Artistic Industries, Monza. This has been fashioned from an iron tube, the dorsal fin being 'pinched' out of the tube. The body is decorated with damascene work in brass, executed by forging. This work is by Antonaci and Martina, students at the Institute.

69.   Julio Gonzales. *Cactus Man*. 1939–1940. Kunsthalle, Hamburg. © by ADAGP, Paris. A native of Catalonia, Julio Gonzales (1876–1942) arrived in Paris at the beginning of the century. He met and influenced Picasso, who learned from Gonzales the expressive potential of iron sculpture.

70.   Julio Gonzales. *Woman Combing her Hair*. Musée National d'Art Moderne, Paris. © by ADAGP, Paris. An impressive and amusing work. 'Abstract' though it is, it conveys admirably the concentrated, somewhat angular posture of a

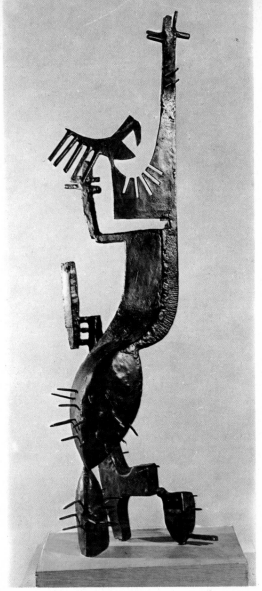

69. Julio Gonzales. *Cactus Man*. 1939–1940.
Kunsthalle, Hamburg.

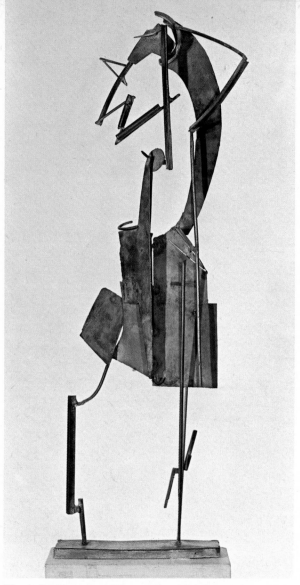

70. Julio Gonzales. *Woman Combing her Hair*.
Musée National d'Art Moderne, Paris.

success at the 2nd Venice Biennale in 1914, where he exhibited works executed in the most varied techniques: repoussé work, sheet-iron, wrought-iron, iron and glass, clay, leather, wood. Among the innumerable screens and railings that Bellotto has produced is one for Dante's tomb at Ravenna—an important work, austere in design and construction. Also important are his railings in the Piazza S. Lorenzo at Mestre, and the more imposing ones for the Chamber of Commerce.

Alberto Gerardi combines a vigilant sensibility with a perfect sense of proportion, almost endowing the harsh metal with a tactile tenderness. His most celebrated work is the wrought-iron railings executed for the temple of Gethsemane in Palestine, representing a large Crown of Thorns surrounded by symbols of the Passion.

Luigi Matteuci, one of the Italian masters who established themselves at the first Monza Biennales, has produced works of large dimensions for a number of Italian and some Continental towns.

Alberto Calligaris's most significant achievement is the interior gates for the Basilica of St Anthony at

Padua, which demonstrate the range of his different techniques and stylistic preferences.

The Second World War was a severe blow to the revived art of ironwork. Not all the forges were shut, but many smiths became locksmiths, deserted the hammer and anvil for carpentry, or produced balconies, grilles and screens—with standard sections, or by using sheets of metal cut out and put together by electric or hydrogen welding within a framework of almost exclusively geometrical design.

Wrought-ironwork, in the traditional sense of the phrase used in this book, is still made in a few workshops that have become famous and attract the connoisseur. The only possible exceptions to the general decline are Germany and Austria, where villas and houses are still being built in the national style, with encouraging numbers of iron locks, grilles and balustrades. Even furniture in which iron plays a large part is still being produced.

On the other hand, there has been a sudden sympathy for iron on the part of sculptors, who have employed it to create new sculptural forms, particularly those intended to be displayed outdoors—on the exteriors of buildings, on lawns, in gardens and parks. Sculptors who have come to the fore in the post-war period and have worked in iron include: the American Alexander Calder, inventor of the 'mobile'; Ibram Lassaw, who has made filiform constructions for walls and exteriors; the Englishman Lynn Chadwick, with his strange mobile crustaceans in iron and glass; Walter Bodmer, who creates coloured and varnished threads of iron wire; Robert Muller, with his compositions of gears in forged iron; Burla and Giesinger, sculptors in massive ironwork; the Spaniards Ferreira and Chillida; the Italians Gio and Arnaldo Pomodoro, Berto Lardera, Barisani, Guarino, and Benetton.

Technological progress has transformed working methods and furnished new means of treating the metal. Specialists have become divided into two camps. One upholds the tradition of forging iron with anvil and hammer in the fire of the forge; it rejects welding and maintains that welding with brass is fragile and false. The other believes in utilising all the available technical processes, and points out that the great masters of the past have always accepted new techniques; Jean Lamour, for example, employed sheet-iron from the time when it was first produced (1760).

The issue is of course largely irrelevant to the practising ironworker. Antonio Benetton, for example, is a master of all the techniques involved in the artistic working of iron, and uses them according to the requirements of his work; if necessary, he invents new ones. His workshop has advanced equipment, exemplary organisation and a highly-trained staff. Here filiform interior decorations or delicate balustrades can be fashioned; or forging with powerful mechanical hammers; or great blocks of white-hot iron can be beaten on the anvil. With enormous blocks of iron and huge sheets of metal taken from scrapped battleships, Benetton models and constructs gigantic sculptures which are set up in town centres.

All of which goes to prove that innovations in the means of expression are not to be feared, though their limitations must be appreciated. The employment of new technical processes permits the attainment of new artistic goals: art, like life, must evolve.

LIST OF ILLUSTRATIONS   Page

156